Contents

Some words are shown in bold, **like this.** You can find out what they mean by looking in the glossary.

Who was Emily Davison?

Emily Davison wanted to improve the lives of women. She fought so that women would be treated the same as men. She broke the law and put her life in danger for what she believed in.

Emily Davison lived more than 100 years ago.

In 1900, no women could vote to elect the government.

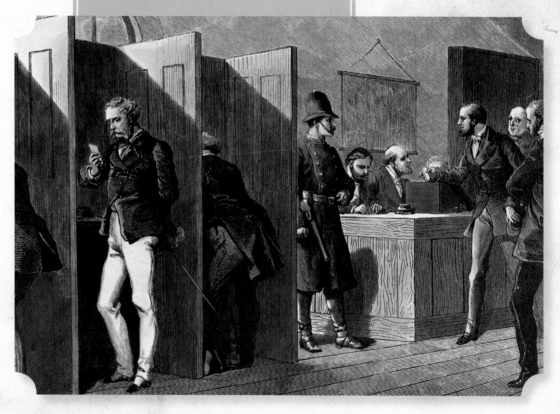

Life for women during Davison's lifetime was very different from today. Men had more **rights** than women, including the right to vote in elections. Davison and other **suffragettes** thought this was wrong.

Who was Rosa Parks?

Rosa Parks risked her life to improve the lives of **African Americans**. Parks believed it was wrong that people like her did not have the same **rights** as white Americans.

Rosa Parks was born in 1913 in the Southern United States.

African Americans were not even allowed to use the same water cooler as their white neighbours.

Life for African Americans was very difficult when Rosa was growing up. In the Southern United States, they were not allowed to go to the same schools or restaurants as white people. This was called **segregation**.

When and where did they grow up?

Emily Davison was born in London on 11 October 1872. Her family was quite wealthy. Emily, her brothers and her sisters were taught at home. Later, Emily went to Kensington High School in London.

In Victorian London, most women from wealthy families did not go out to work.

These students were some of the
first women to have the chance
to study at university.

Emily did well at school and went to
university. Most students were men.
She scored top marks in her exams at
Oxford University, but women were not
awarded degrees like the men.

Rosa McCauley was born near Montgomery, Alabama, USA on 4 February 1913. She went to several local schools. Rosa had to leave school early to care for her mother and grandmother, who were ill.

When Rosa was growing up, many poor people relied on buses and streetcars to travel around the city.

African American children could not go to the same schools as white children.

Schools were not the only places that were **segregated** in Alabama. While white American children could travel to school by bus, **African Americans** like Rosa had to walk.

11

Getting involved

Davison became a **governess**, teaching the children of a wealthy family. She then worked as a teacher at a school in Birmingham. In the early 1900s, educated women did not have many jobs to choose from.

Emily Davison finally gained her degree from the University of London in 1908.

Protests were organized to win the **right** for women to vote, like this one in 1912.

Many people thought that women were treated unfairly in society. Davison joined the Women's Social and Political Union in 1906. They organized protests in favour of votes for women.

13

Rosa married Raymond Parks in 1932. Raymond was a member of the **NAACP**, a group that wanted to make the lives of **African Americans** better. He encouraged Rosa to get involved too.

After her marriage, Rosa returned to finish high school.

African Americans protested peacefully to be treated as equals.

Parks became secretary of her local branch of the NAACP. It was dangerous work. People who took part in **campaigns** for **civil rights** could be attacked or even killed by those who did not want a fair society.

What did they do?

Davison became a **suffragette**. Many suffragettes believed in breaking the law to win more **rights** for women. Davison even used violence, and many suffragettes disagreed with her extreme ideas.

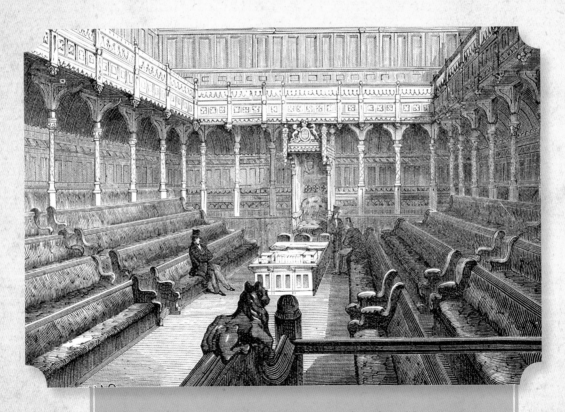

In 1911, Davison hid inside the Houses of Parliament. Women could not become **Members of Parliament** until 1918.

Suffragettes risked being arrested to draw attention to their beliefs.

Davison was sent to prison several times because of her protests, along with other suffragettes. She refused to eat food. This was her way of complaining about the way the suffragettes were being treated.

On 1 December 1955, Parks caught the bus after work. The driver asked her to give up her seat so a white passenger could sit down. Parks refused, and was arrested for breaking a law on **segregation**.

Parks was **fined** for not giving up her seat on the bus.

African Americans **boycotted** the buses in Montgomery, Alabama for more than a year.

Parks's refusal to move was supported by other **African Americans**. They refused to use the city's buses. Finally, the **US Supreme Court** decided that segregation on buses was against the law.

Fighting for freedom

On 4 June 1913, Davison ran out on to the track during the Derby horse race. She tried to grab the horse owned by King George V, but she was knocked to the ground and badly injured.

The race was filmed and people across the country saw Davison's protest.

"The Suffragette," June 13, 1913. Registered at the G.P.O. as a Newspaper

The **Suffragette**

Edited by Christabel Pankhurst.

The Official Organ of the
Women's Social and Political Union

No. 35—Vol. 1.   FRIDAY, JUNE 13, 1913.   Price 1d. Weekly (Post Free)

LOVE THAT OVERCOMETH

IN HONOUR AND IN LOVING, REVERENT MEMORY
OF
EMILY WILDING DAVISON.
SHE DIED FOR WOMEN.

"Greater love hath no man than this, that he lay down his life for his friends."

Davison, who made a protest at the Derby against the denial of Votes to Women, was knocked down by the King's horse and sustained terrible injuries of which she died on Sunday, June 8th, 1913.

The *Suffragette* magazine praised Davison's courage.

Davison died from her injuries four days after the Derby. She died for her cause, but no one knows if she meant to die in her protest. Many people think that she was trying to attach a flag to the horse.

After her brave protest in Montgomery, Parks found life difficult. She was a hero to **African Americans**, but she lost her job and had to move house to find work.

Parks moved to the city of Detroit in 1957.

Parks received the Congressional Gold Medal in 1999.

Parks was famous, but she was never rich. African Americans continued their battle to have the same **rights** as white people. Quietly, Parks worked the rest of her life for the cause of **civil rights**.

How did they change the world?

Davison's death was reported around the world. More people learned about women's struggle to be allowed to vote. Many other women chose peaceful ways to protest.

Even though some British women were allowed to vote in 1918, many continued to protest for equal **rights** with men in other areas of life.

Women began to work in factories when men went to fight in World War I.

Between 1914 and 1918, women workers helped to win World War I. The wartime changes and the protests of **suffragettes** like Davison changed people's minds. Some women were allowed to vote in 1918.

Parks's refusal to move from her seat on the bus inspired many people. Many others risked arrest or violence to protest peacefully. Parks was called the "Mother of the **Civil Rights** Movement".

Parks with Martin Luther King, another well-known leader of the civil rights struggle.

In April 2012, President Obama visited the Henry Ford Museum in Detroit. He sat on the same bus that Parks had travelled on back in 1955.

During the 1960s, the protests won equal **rights** for **African Americans**. Parks died in 2005. Four years after her death, Barack Obama became the first African American President of the United States.

Comparing Emily Davison

Emily Davison

Born | 11 October 1872

Died | 8 June 1913

Career

Governess and teacher, before becoming a full-time worker for the Women's Social and Political Union

Fascinating fact

Davison was sent to prison seven times for protests, including setting fire to postboxes.

Famous people living at the same time

Edith Cavell (nurse and World War I heroine, 1865–1915)

Emmeline Pankhurst (leader of the **suffragettes**, 1858–1928)

Mohandas Gandhi (Indian independence **campaigner**, 1869–1948)

1750   1800   1850   1900

and Rosa Parks

Rosa Parks

Born 4 February 1913

Died 24 October 2005

Career

Held several jobs including seamstress and working for a politician; a campaigner for **civil rights** throughout her life

Fascinating fact

In 1995, Parks was awarded the Presidential Medal of Freedom by US President Bill Clinton.

Famous people living at the same time

Nelson Mandela (political campaigner and President of South Africa, 1918–2013)
Martin Luther King (civil rights campaigner, 1929–1968)
Mother Teresa (Christian missionary and carer for the poor, 1910–1997)

Glossary

African American American citizen whose ancestors were brought to North America from Africa as slaves

boycott refuse to use something, as a form of protest

campaign a series of aggressive activities to achieve a specific purpose

civil rights rights of people to take part in society and politics without being treated unfairly, whatever their gender, race or religion

fine charge a sum of money as a penalty for wrongdoing

governess woman who teaches children in a private household

Member of Parliament someone who is elected to sit in parliament and helps to make laws

NAACP National Association for the Advancement of Colored People, US organization that tried to win equal rights for African Americans

right something people are entitled to that is protected by law in a society, like the freedom to live in peace

segregation separating groups of people according to their race

suffragette woman who tried to gain more rights for other women through protest

US Supreme Court highest court of law in the United States

Find out more

Books

Rosa Parks and the Montgomery Bus Boycott (Graphic History), Connie Colwell Miller (Raintree, 2012)

Suffragette (My Story), Carol Drinkwater (Scholastic, 2011)

Women Who Changed History, Adam Sutherland (Wayland, 2013)

Women Win the Vote (Dates With History), Brian Williams (Cherrytree Books, 2009)

Websites

www.biography.com/people/rosa-parks-9433715

This website includes a video about Rosa Parks's life.

www.britishpathe.com/video/emily-davison-throws-herself-under-the-kings-derby

Here you can see the original film of Emily Davison's final protest in 1913, with more recent commentary.

http://memory.loc.gov/ammem/today/dec01.html

There are important documents from Parks's life on this website.

Index